SHOTGUNS

SHOTGUNS

Philip Schreier & Jim Supica

Produced by TAJ Books International LLP
27, Ferndown Gardens,
Cobham,
Surrey,
UK,
KT11 2BH
www.tajbooks.com

Company history text supplied by Karen Vellucci

Photos courtesy of Philip Schreier: page 8, 9, 11, 13, 14, 16 & 17, 18 & 19
Photo courtesy of Andrea Cerwinske: page 20

You can join the NRA by contacting them at:

The National Rifle Association of America
11250 Waples Mill Road
Fairfax VA 22030

or by visiting their website, www.nra.org

And you can view the treasures of the NRA National Firearms Museum at the website
www.nramuseum.org.

The museum is open every day of the week, except major holidays, at NRA Headquarters in Fairfax VA, near
Washington DC. There is no admission charge.

All notations of errors or omissions should be addressed to Thunder Bay Press, Editorial Department, at the
above address. All other correspondence (author inquiries, permissions) concerning the content of this book
should be addressed to TAJ Books, 27, Ferndown Gardens, Cobham, Surrey, UK, KT11 2BH, info@tajbooks.com.

ISBN-13: 978-1-84406-150-1

Library of Congress Cataloging-in-Publication Data available on request.

Printed in China.

1 2 3 4 5 14 13 12 11 10

CONTENTS

Introduction

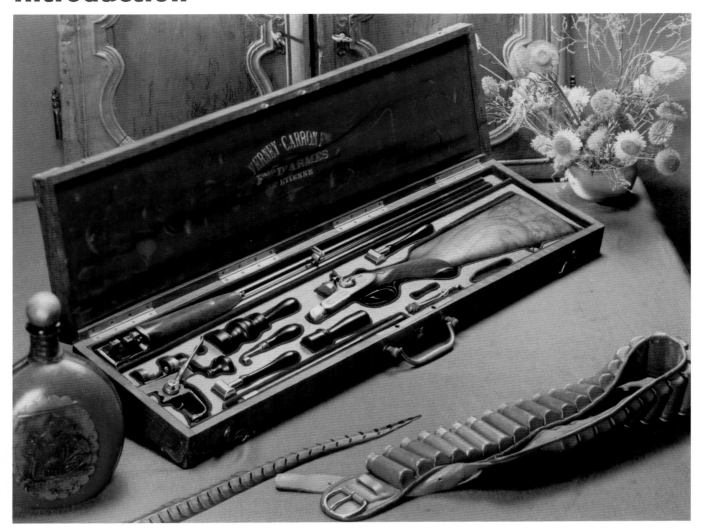

An antique Verney Carron Shotgun in its original case.

A History of Shotguns

As long as man has used tools, weapons have been among those of foremost importance. They have been used to provide food and protection since the formation of the earliest social units.

For centuries, and continuing through today, men and women have used firearms as the most effective weapons individuals can wield. Guns have been used to implement both the highest and basest goals of humanity: to put food on the table, to provide personal protection, to enforce or defy the law, to defend or acquire territory and treasure, and to liberate or to enslave.

Guns have also come to be used for a wide variety of recreational and competitive shooting, and millions of Americans exercise their constitutional right to own firearms simply for the pleasure of shooting or the enjoyment of ownership.

Shotguns have evolved from the earliest known projectile firing devices, becoming the world's most elaborately engraved and embellished, and therefore some of the most expensive firearms.

Today, shotguns are used for hunting, sporting games, as well as serving vital roles in military and law enforcement use.

Earliest Firearms

The origin of gunpowder is unknown, and may have occurred in China, Turkey, or Europe. The first record describing the combination of charcoal, sulphur, and saltpeter, to produce a rapidly burning or exploding powder is a coded writing by Franciscan monk Roger Bacon shortly before 1250 AD.

Within fifty years, early cannons had been developed. A large, thick metal tube with one closed end (the breech) and an open end (the muzzle) was loaded first with gunpowder and then with a projectile. The powder was ignited with a torch or smoldering ember through a small hole in the rear (the touch hole). The rapidly expanding gases from the exploding gunpowder would throw the projectile from the barrel. This basic principle still applies today.

It took another half century for this concept to be applied to individual handheld weapons. The first firearms, ca. 1350, called "hand cannons" or "hand gonnes" were essentially miniature cannons designed to be held by hand or attached to a pole for use by individual soldiers. They were loaded and fired in the same manner as the full-size cannons.

Early Ignition Systems

For the next four centuries, the greatest advances in the evolution of firearms would focus primarily on the search for more reliable methods of igniting the gunpowder, in addition to design advances for more rapid repeat shots and better accuracy.

The term "lock, stock, and barrel" comes from firearms design, representing the three major components of early guns. The barrel is self-explanatory, and the stock is of course the wooden holder in which the barrel is mounted, allowing the gun to be fired from the shoulder or from one hand. The lock is the mechanical contrivance that is used to ignite the charge of gunpowder in the chamber of the barrel.

The first gun to combine all three components was the matchlock, in the early 1400s. Many early hand cannons were ignited with a "slow match"—a length of slender rope or cord that had been chemically treated so that an end could be ignited and would continue to burn or smolder, much like a punk used to shoot fireworks. Obviously it was awkward to hold both

An example of an AYA No. 1 and No. 2 Shotgun.

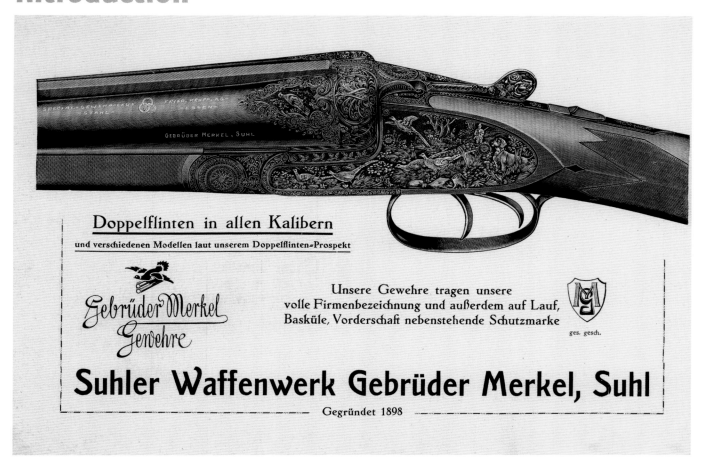

An original advertisement for an early Merkel shotgun in 1898.

both gun and slow match while trying to dip the match to the touch hole of the hand cannon.

The matchlock solved this problem by using an arm called a serpentine on the gun to hold the slow match. By mechanical linkage, a trigger mounted on the bottom of the lock could be pressed to lower the match to the touch hole, which now included a small pan of fine gunpowder that would be ignited first, transmitting the fire through the hole to fire the main charge in the barrel.

This simple system was followed by a much more complicated one, the wheellock in the early 1500s. It was the first to take advantage of the fact that sparks could be produced by striking flint or other substances against steel. The lock contained a wheel with a serrated edge, attached to a spring that could be wound with a separate key called a spanner, much like early clocks, and held under tension. A hammer-like piece called the dogshead held a piece of pyrite rock. To fire a wheellock, the dogshead was lowered onto the edge of the wheel, which was released by a pull of the trigger causing a shower of sparks to fall into the pan and igniting the charge. The principle is much the same as a cigarette lighter.

This was an improvement in reliability over the matchlock, primarily because the shooter did not have to constantly attend to the smoldering slow match to ensure that it remained lit. It also avoided the problem of an enemy seeing—or game smelling—the smoke of the match before the gun was fired. However, it

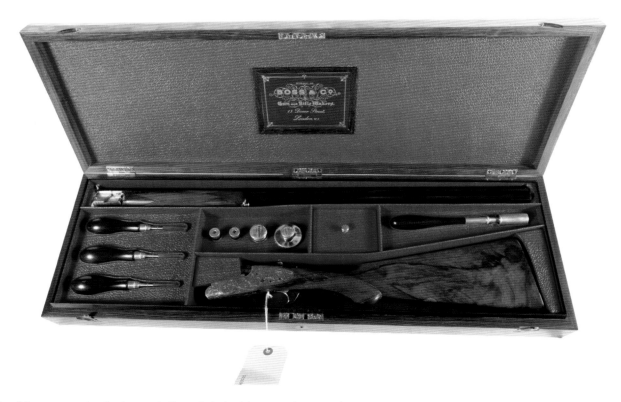

Considered by many to be the finest of all English double guns, this Boss & Co. 12 ga is cased with all required accoutrements. Boss & Co. was established in 1812.

took highly skilled craftsmen to build the clocklike mechanism of the wheellock, making it an extremely expensive piece, primarily available to royalty and the like for hunting. Although wheellocks saw some military use, the matchlock remained the most common military firearm during the wheellock era.

One of today's premier gunmakers can trace its roots to this era. Beretta began operations in Brescia, Italy, in 1526, making it one of the oldest industrial companies in the world. Today, Beretta manufactures some of the world's finest shotguns and owns the Franchi, Stoeger, and Benelli companies, who make world-class shotguns in their own right.

Flintlocks

Improvements using flint against steel to provide the igniting spark continued in the second half of the sixteenth century, with two early examples being the snaphaunce, the first flintlock-type gun ca. 1560, and the Miquelet, following a couple decades later.

The snaphaunce held a piece of flint in the hammer-like cock, with a pan of priming powder mounted on the outside of the barrel over the touch hole as with the matchlock system. When ready to fire, a steel striking plate (the "battery") would be manually swiveled into place above the pan, and the cock pulled back until it was caught by a sear. Pulling the trigger would release the cock to swing rapidly forward, striking the battery and showering sparks into the pan, hopefully firing the gun.

As with all flintlock-type systems, sometimes the priming powder in the pan would ignite, but would fail to transmit the fire to the powder in the barrel resulting in a failure to fire, and giving us a colorful phrase still used today: "a flash in the pan."

Of course, it was also vital to "keep your powder dry," and accordingly many early firearms of this era had a sliding pan cover to hold the powder in place and give it some protection against the elements. The pan cover would have to be manually swiveled out of the way before firing.

Around 1580 the Miquelet system improved on and simplified the snaphaunce by combining the battery and pan cover into a single piece, called the frizzen. This L-shaped spring-loaded piece would be pivoted down to cover the pan after it had been primed with powder. When the cock was released by the trigger, it would swing forward striking the frizzen, producing sparks at the same time it pushed the frizzen up and forward to expose the powder in the pan to the igniting sparks.

In the early 1600s, the basic design of the flintlock, originally known as the French lock, was perfected. The major improvement over the Miquelet consisted of moving the mechanical components for the lock mechanism from their previous position on the outside of the lockplate, where they were exposed to elements and damage to the interior of the lock.

Improvements In Accuracy

At around the time flintlock systems were first being developed, two improvements were introduced that dramatically increased the accuracy of firearms. Archers had found that if the fletching feathers on the rear of their arrow were at a slight angle, causing the arrow to rotate in flight, and their ability to hit the target was improved. This concept was applied to gun barrels by cutting slightly twisting grooves down the

The cased Merkel 2 barreled 12 ga shotgun of German Reichsmarschall Hermann Göring, presented to him in 1937 at his Carinhall estate.

Introduction

A close-up of the detail on a Churchill Hercules.

interior length of the barrel, imparting a spin to the bullet as it left the muzzle. These grooves were called rifling, and rifled guns were found to be much better at hitting their mark over farther distances than those with "smooth bores."

With the improved accuracy offered by rifled firearms, a system of aiming them other than pointing became more important, and early forms of sights became more widely used. A common system, still used on most handguns today, was a notch of some type at the rear of the barrel and a post on the front. With this type of open sight, the top of the front sight post is aligned with the target, and the post is centered by eye between the edges of the rear sight notch, with the top of the post level with the tops of the sides of the notch. When the sights themselves are properly physically aligned with the axis of the bore, this system still provides all the accuracy required for most practical shooting needs.

Each of these early forms of firearms can be found in both handgun and long gun configurations.

The Percussion System

Although the flintlock system predominated in firearms production for nearly two centuries, problems remained. A shooter often had to carry two types of powder—fine grained for priming and coarse for the main charge, and the system was unreliable in wet weather. It was difficult to store a gun loaded and ready for use.

In 1807 a Scottish clergyman, Reverand Alexander John Forsyth, is credited with developing an ignition system based on the principle that certain chemicals would ignite with a spark when struck with a sharp blow—a concept which can be observed in toy cap pistols or "pop rock" fireworks today. Various methods to utilize this approach were tried, and in 1822 the percussion cap was invented.

The percussion cap contains a small charge of chemical in a small copper cuplike holder that can be quickly pressed onto to a nipple mounted in the rear of a gun barrel. When the trigger is pulled, the hammer strikes the cap, igniting the chemical, which sparks through a hole in the nipple into the main charge in the barrel, firing the gun. This system offered such obvious advantages to the flintlock method that gunmakers around the world rapidly adapted their existing designs to percussion ignition, although within fifty years of accelerating firearms evolution, it too, would be obsolete.

Repeaters And Breechloaders

The introduction of the percussion system marks the beginning of a dramatically rapid era of firearms advancements, coinciding with the Industrial Revolution and including the era of the American Civil War, through the turn of the century. During this relatively brief time, guns would go from primitive flintlocks to the basic systems that still dominate firearms designs today.

Development of effective breechloading systems was one of these concepts. From the matchlock through the early percussion era, the vast majority of guns had been "muzzleloaders." That is, the powder and projectile had to be dropped down the muzzle at the front of the barrel, and rammed to the rear before firing. This made reloading awkward, especially if trying to shoot a long gun from a prone position or

The John Browning–designed Winchester 1897.

Introduction

Close-up of the detailing on the side of a Beretta 471.

behind cover or concealment, and, as noted earlier, became more difficult after a few shots when barrel fouling made the job more strenuous. This led to many attempts to develop a gun that loaded from the rear of the barrel, although most early efforts were not effective due to weakness of materials and the leakage of hot gases from the breech seal when the gun was fired.

An even more pressing concern was the relatively long time it took to reload a firearm, and the need for rapid follow-up shots. An archer could loose several arrows in the time it took a "musketeer" to reload after he had fired his weapon.

In even the earliest days of firearms design, this could be addressed in a limited manner by mounting multiple barrels (and usually multiple locks) onto the same stock. This basic concept is still in use today, in the double barrel shotguns produced by some of the finest gun makers in the world, including firms such as Browning, Franchi, Beretta, Remington, Ruger, and Charles Daly, and is a system preferred by many discriminating hunters and competitive shooters.

Ammunition developments in the mid-1800s would drive the evolution of shotguns for the next century. The two most significant developments would be the self-contained cartridge and smokeless powder as a propellant.

The Self-Contained Cartridge

What was needed to really expand the use and practicality of shotguns was a self-contained cartridge with the primer, powder, and shot all in one neat and weatherproof unit.

An early attempt at this was the pinfire system, first introduced around 1846, in which a firing pin was mounted on each copper-cased cartridge, igniting an internal primer when struck by the gun's hammer. Although it gained a good deal of popularity in Europe, it never caught on much in the United States, with the external pin on each round being a bit cumbersome and hazardous.

The American development of the self-contained metallic cartridge by Smith & Wesson in the 1850s led to advancements in rimfire priming systems that eventually evolved into the centerfire cartridge we still use today. Shotgun shells were first constructed out of waxed paper with brass or copper bases and eventually developed into the plastic-tubed, brass-based shells still in use. Solid brass shells have been in use, mostly by military and law enforcement for high-powered loads since the early 1900s.

Smokeless Powder

Smokeless powder, as the name implies, had the military advantage of not generating a cloud of smoke when fired. Black powder smoke would reveal a shooter's position visually and, after a few rounds, develop a haze that could begin to obscure his vision. Another advantage was that smokeless powder produced far less fouling after shots than black powder, meaning that more shots could be fired before cleaning, and that powder debris was less likely to clog.

Its most important quality, however, was that when ignited, its gases would expand more rapidly, creating higher pressures and driving the bullet to a higher velocity when it left the muzzle. As a bullet approaches 2,000 feet per second (about the speed of sound), its wounding capacity increases dramatically, allowing a lighter, smaller diameter projectile to have the same "stopping power" as a larger, heavier round at a slower speed.

In general terms, the caliber of a bullet refers to a rough measurement of its diameter, expressed either in decimal fractions of an inch or millimeters. For example, a .45 caliber cartridge takes a bullet approximately 45/100" in diameter, which would also be very roughly 11 mm in diameter.

Shotgun projectiles are called shot or pellets. There are anywhere from one to hundreds of "shot" in a shotgun shell. Shot is lead or steel balls loaded on top of a cushion, or "wad" that buffers the shot from the propellant or powder. The largest shot is a rifled slug

The John Browning–designed Winchester 1887 lever-action shotgun.

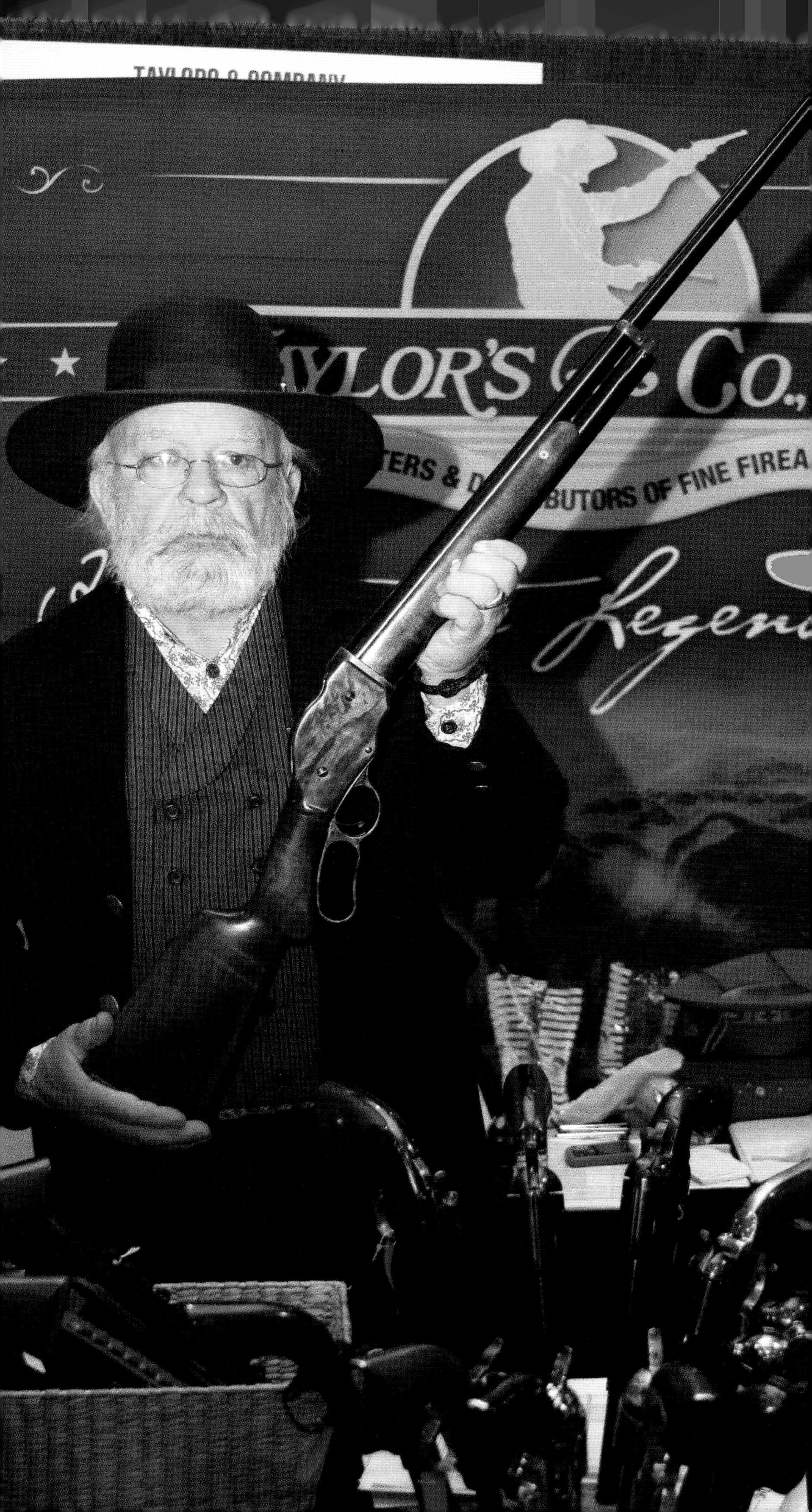
YLOR'S Co.,
TERS & D BUTORS OF FINE FIREA

Introduction

A modern Thompson Centre Endevour competition shotgun.

the same diameter of the bore of the gun. These rifled slugs are used to generally hunt large game in areas where rifles are prohibited due to their long ranges. Shot then ranges in various sizes measured from BB, B, 1, 2, 3, 4, 5, 6, 7 ½, 8, 8 ½, 9, and "chilled shot," which is almost sand like. BB shot has approximately fifty round balls of equal diameter per ounce. The higher the shot size, the smaller the shot. Number 9 shot has approximately 600 same-diameter balls per ounce.

While rifles and pistols use the same measuring system, 1/100 of an inch, to determine caliber, shotguns are measured by gauge. Gauge refers to the diameter of the bore measured by the number of round lead balls equal to the diameter that would weigh a pound when weighed together. In other words, a 12-gauge shotgun has a bore diameter the same size of the diameter of twelve lead balls that weigh a pound. The actual diameter of a 12-gauge would be .72 caliber if it was measured like a rifle or pistol. Common gauges of shotguns in the last century have been 8, 10, 12, 16, 20, and 28. The only exception to this rule is the .410 gauge, the smallest shotgun gauge. The .410 gauge is actually a caliber and not a gauge as the diameter is measured in 1/100 of an inch.

Shotguns in the American West

The American West of 1865 to 1900 is perhaps one of the most popular and romanticized eras of American history, with the lore of cowboy and Indian, lawman and outlaw, figuring large in our collective imagination. There are many who say that the Winchester was the rifle that won the West and the Colt was the pistol that won the West. But when you look at sheer numbers and incidents of use, the gun that truly settled the west was the old Damascus-barreled side-by-side scattergun. Every pioneer who headed west traveled with a shotgun (at the very least) to find and provide sustenance for his family and himself. It was an effective defensive weapon as well, with just the simple act of displaying a shotgun ending many an argument before they began.

Birth of the Modern Shotgun

The modern industrial age began in the mid-1800s and brought about many changes to everyday life, which has since been known as the Industrial Revolution to place its significance in a proper light. With the age of machines and factories came increases in workers' wages, as well as products for them to consume with their new wealth. Additionally, the spread of railroads throughout the countryside opened up vast areas to sport hunting that had been previously impractical for the average hunter/sportsman to enjoy. As machines sped up the production of manufactured goods, they became cheaper to obtain and soon the middle class began to afford not only finer grade firearms, but ones designed specifically for sporting use, and not just for sustenance as had previously been the case. Self-contained cartridges gave birth to the era of the breechloader and with the new design out pacing muzzle loaders by the 1860s, new patents on firearms designs were taken out almost weekly in both the United States and Great Britain. During this period, most shotguns were made with twist steel or Damascus steel, and fired by two external hammers, sometimes called "rabbit ears" in relaxed company.

In 1875 two employees of the Westley Richards and Co. of Birmingham, England, William Anson and John Deeley, patented a revolutionary lock mechanism that changed the look and function of shotguns forever. The Anson and Deeley boxlock used an internal cocking system that eliminated the exposed hammers. The boxlock and subsequent sidelock are still the standard lock systems used with side-by-side and over-and-under-shotguns.

Early Auto-Loaders

A firearms design trend in Europe given a boost by the introduction of smokeless powder was the attempt to make automatic loading firearms. In general, gun

Sergeant Johnson of Task Force Gladius holds a U.S. Military Mossberg Model 550 in Afghanistan, in August 2009.

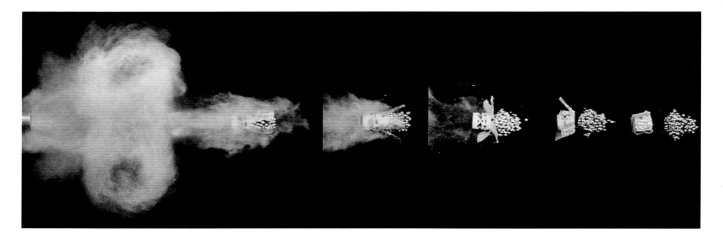

Series of individual 1/1,000,000 second exposures showing shotgun firing shot and sabot separation.

designs to this point had relied on some mechanical action by the shooter to load a fresh cartridge into the firing chamber after the initial round had been fired, whether it was swiveling a lever; lifting, pulling, and pushing a bolt; or cocking the hammer or pulling the trigger to advance a revolver cylinder to the next chamber. Inventors sought a method whereby the loading of the next round would be accomplished automatically.

John Moses Browning

At this point in the history of firearms, we must travel back across the Atlantic, and back a few years in time to track the career of probably the greatest firearms inventor of all time, John Moses Browning of Ogden, Utah. Browning was a prolific inventor and innovator, and his designs for lever-action rifles, single-shot rifles, and shotguns are still being produced today.

Browning was responsible for some of the first repeating shotguns. Revolver-based shotguns had been around since the Colt Paterson models of the 1840s, but had never caught on (probably because of the tendency of hot gases escaping from the cylinder gap to pepper the supporting hand with powder grains). Spencer Arms (of Civil War lever-action rifle

The 12 ga side-by-side was the most used gun in the American West.

fame) had manufactured a moderately successful repeating pump or slide-action shotgun as early as 1882. As would befit the Winchester legacy, Browning's first design for a repeating shotgun for that firm was a lever-action, the Model 1887. This was followed by a pump-action Model 1893, which would be modified to become the highly successful Model 1897.

Browning's auto-loading designs were not limited to handguns, rifles, and machine guns. His "humpback" Auto 5 shotgun was a tremendous success, popular still today, and has been made by Fabrique National, Remington, and Browning.

Class III (NFA) Shotguns

In most states, short-barreled shotguns can be legally owned by private citizens, although they must be registered with the government and are closely regulated. Based on the names of the laws that regulate them, they're sometimes called "NFA" (National Firearms Act) or "Class III" firearms. Their primary uses are for recreational shooting in a safe well-supervised setting, and have a dedicated following of collectors.

Chokes

When you look at a shotgun for sale, most will list the length of the barrels and the chokes. The length of a shotgun barrel will have a great effect on how the pattern of shot is dispersed over distance once fired. The longer the barrel, the tighter the pattern, or spray, of pellets. Shorter barrels tend to allow the shot (pellets) to spread out quicker and wider at closer ranges. Altering the muzzle end of the shotgun barrel to affect the pattern of shot is called choking. Modern chokes were developed by an American, Joseph Smith of Rhode Island in 1827. W. W. Greener and William Pape of England are credited with standardizing and developing the modern method of choking shotguns in 1866.

Today most shotguns come with interchangeable chokes, allowing the shooter the opportunity of switching chokes depending on the sport or type of game he is shooting.

Chokes today come in six different diameters. From the widest to the tightest they are: Cylinder, Skeet, Improved Cylinder, Modified, Improved Modified, and Full. Cylinder is considered an open bore choke giving the shot the widest pattern the shortest distance from the muzzle. Full choke is the tightest giving the shooter greater range with the most concentration of shot.

Introduction

A U.S. Special Forces soldier holds a US M 4 Benelli Super 90 shotgun in Afghanistan, in August 2009.

Modern Shotgun Milestones

Recent decades have witnessed the continuing evolution and development of other types of sporting firearms, with several recurring trends.

The trend to new materials other than traditional blue steel and wood began years in the post–World War II years. Today shotgun stocks are available in many types of synthetic materials with some shotguns used for turkey and deer hunting, completely camouflaged from muzzle to buttplate.

In the repeating shotgun field, the Winchester Model 12 became probably the standard for pump shotguns in the mid-twentieth century, perhaps replaced by the Remington Model 870 in more recent years. Semiauto shotguns have overcome their reputation for finicky performance, first with Remington 1100, and then the Benelli Model 90, enjoying an outstanding reputation for reliability in recent years.

Probably the last of the great firearms inventors in the tradition of Sam Colt and D. B. Wesson was Bill Ruger. His Sturm, Ruger firm developed a reputation for improving classic sporting gun designs, and turning out a broad line of well-made and reasonably priced firearms, from revolvers and rifles through auto-pistols and over-under shotguns.

Shotgunning Today

Shotgunning today enjoys many forms: sporting games such as trap and skeet, Olympic competition, hunting, military, and collecting. Each pursuit employs different styles of shotguns made by a wide variety of manufacturers. Some makers specialize in specific types made for a limited market while others mass-produce shotguns of numerous designs and styles for a wide variety of uses.

Sporting Games

With the advent of leisure pursuits in the mid-1800s, sporting games became vogue among the upper classes of society. At first, shooters would shoot live birds, penned and the released by a chucker. Then the development of the clay pigeon at the turn of the nineteenth century eliminated live bird shooting but many of the terms and calls used on a skeet or trap field still refer to the age when real birds were used.

Skeet shooting is a sport where a shooter stands in one of eight stations that form a semi-circle and takes turns shooting at clay birds "thrown" from either a high house (left side) or a low house (right side). A double-barreled shotgun or a semiautomatic with 26" or 28" and variable chokes is most commonly used in skeet.

Trap shooting is done alternately from each of five positions behind a trap house and the birds fly away from the shooter at various angles and heights. Longer-barreled guns (28"–32") and tighter chokes are

generally used in trap. There are numerous Olympic medal events in both trap and skeet and they are among the oldest medal sports since the inception of the modern Olympics in 1896.

Variations of trap and skeet are quite popular today with sporting clays, five stand, wobble trap, and a host of other variations of the same themes finding new fans among today's sportsmen who are looking for new challenges.

Hunting

Shotguns enjoy a wide variety of uses in the hunting fields. Spring and fall turkey hunting is one of the most popular and has seen the most changes in style and form of shotguns in recent years. Some makers produce shotguns completely camouflaged to give the hunter the advantage of concealment in the fields.

Some semiautos and pump shotguns are made so the barrels can be removed and switched with a specialized barrel for hunting deer. These barrels have rifle-type sights and may even sport a scope.

Upland game hunting and waterfowl also require specialized firearms designed with unique features meant to aid the hunter in their quest for game.

Military Uses

The U.S. military has used shotguns since the founding of the nation in 1775. The military shotgun is a very effective way of discharging a great number of lethal projectiles over a wide pattern at close ranges. John Browning's 1897 Winchester pump-action 12-gauge is perhaps the best known of all the U.S. military shotguns and was used with great effect in both world wars of the twentieth century. Its devastatingly effective use by U.S. Marines in the trenches of the Western Front in 1918 gave the Germans cause to nickname the Marines "teufelhunden" which translates to "Devil Dogs."

Collecting

The rich history of shotguns has given the collector a vast area to research and collect. Some collectors only collect shotguns of a specific gauge while others collect specific types, such as military or English sporting guns. Some find great beauty in Damascus barreled guns made before World War I. Others collect the finest made by specific manufacturers such as Parker Brothers or Ithaca, some of the finest American makers.

Shotguns made for royalty and historic figures can often bring hundreds of thousands of dollars. Of all the American shotgun makers, Parker Brothers is often considered one of the finest in craftsmanship. Of the nine grades of quality made by Parker Brothers, the highest was known as the Invincible, of which only three were ever made. All three are on exhibit at the National Rifle Association's (NRA) National Firearms Museum in Fairfax, Virginia, and are valued at over one million dollars each due to their station as the three finest American made shotguns in history.

Introduction

A Stoeger Condor with alternative barrel.

Enjoying Firearms

Firearms ownership and usage is a treasured American tradition. There are two fundamental requirements for those who would participate in this experience.

The first is of course safety. Everyone needs to know the basic safety rules by heart. There are many, but the following, if committed to memory and followed religiously, will prevent tragic mishaps:

1. Treat every firearm as if it is loaded.
2. Never let the muzzle point at anything you are not willing to see destroyed.
3. Do not touch the trigger until your sights are on target.
4. Be sure of your target, and what is beyond it. Firearms projectiles can travel long distances, and will penetrate many visual barriers.
5. Keep your firearms so they are not accessible to unauthorized, untrained, or irresponsible individuals.

Even folks who choose not to own guns need to be sure their children understand basic gun safety. For the smallest kids, the National Rifle Association (NRA's) Eddy Eagle program has a basic, easy to remember drill for what they should do if they come across a gun:

1. Stop!
2. Don't touch.
3. Leave the area.
4. Tell an adult.

No one is born knowing how to shoot. If you choose to own a firearm, get instruction in how to use it safely and effectively. Even if you don't own a gun, such training can still be a good idea, as it may someday be as vital to you or a loved one as is training in CPR.

The NRA is the largest firearms training organization in the world, and offers solid programs for folks from beginning to advanced shooters. Ask a local gun shop, gun club, shooting range, or police department to put you in touch with an NRA certified program.

This brings us to the second requirement for firearms owner: vigilance.

There is a special genius to the Bill of Rights of the U.S. Constitution, which protects the individual and collective civil rights of Americans. It is no mistake that the second amendment to that document provides that ". . . the right of the people to keep and bear arms shall not be infringed."

If it were not for the National Rifle Association, that basic human right would have been lost long ago. It's an ongoing battle; not always an easy or popular one, but an essential one nonetheless.

A prospective customer examines a selection of fine English doubles.

A Franchi 48AL Upland shotgun.

Baikal

Baikal—Federal State Unitary Plant "IZHEVSKY MEKHANICHESKY ZAVOD" (FSUP "IMZ")—is one of the largest businesses within the Russian Agency on Conventional Armament.

In 1944 the first production facility went into operation, producing motorcycles, mining equipment, and scales.

From 1945 to 1955, the company produced more than 5 million of the new army Makarov pistols, one of the best of its kind. Also during this period, in 1949, the company began the manufacture of the ZK simple single-barrel model and the IZH-49 double-barrel gun. The Baikal plant became one of the largest manufacturers of sporting and hunting guns in the world.

An important hallmark not only for the company but also for firearms manufacturing in general was the 1956 opening of the Gunsmithing and Engraving School to train qualified gun makers.

The intervening decades were devoted to the production of a wide range of firearms and other products for the Soviet military. The number of government orders greatly decreased by 1990, and Baikal turned its attention to increasing its manufacture and types of hunting, sporting, and personal firearms.

In the 1990s, Baikal for the first time was able to export products to the United States. The legendary Makarov pistol was replaced by the 9 mm Yarygin army pistol in 2000. Today Baikal firearms are available in more than sixty-five countries.

MP-18E "Sporting" Single-Barrel Gun

MP-18M-M Single-Barrel Gun

MP-18 "Junior" Single-Barrel Gun

MP-27E-1C "Sporting" Double-Barrel Gun

MP-27 Double-Barrel
Over-under Gun

MP-27 "Junior"
Double-Barrel Gun

Baikal

MP-39 Double-Barrel Gun

MP-43 Side-by-side Shotgun

MP-43KH Side-by-side Hammer Shotgun

MP-153 Semiauto-matic Shotgun for Practical Shooting

MP-133 Pump-Action Single-Barrel Gun showing with stock and pistol grip

Benelli

Founded in 1967, the Italian arms manufacturer, Benelli Armi, is located in Urbino, Italy. The six Benelli brothers were famous for Fratelli Benelli, a company founded in 1911 to produce motorcycles. By 1967, the Benelli brothers' passion for hunting had led them from motorcycles to the production of a quality automatic shotgun capable of firing five rounds per second, making it the fastest gun in the world. The concept and development of this revolutionary firearm was the work of designer Bruno Civolani who created a unique inertia system which remains the basis for many of the Benelli guns produced today.

The firm is world renowned for superior shotguns favored by military, law enforcement, and civilians. Many United States SWAT teams prefer the Benelli M3 12-gauge. In recent years, Benelli developed the Benelli M4 Super 90, a remarkable gas-operated semiautomatic shotgun designed for military use in urban settings. In 2000 Pietro Benelli became the owner of Benelli and Benelli USA.

A favorite choice for waterfowl hunters is the Benelli Super Black Eagle, one of the first semiautomatic shotguns capable of firing the 2.75, 3, and 3.5-inch shotgun shells. In 1993 Tom Knapp, recognized as one of the foremost exhibition shooters of today, joined Team Benelli, a group of professional shooters who use only Benelli firearms. Knapp holds three world shooting records for handheld clay targets. His most recent record was set in October 2004 when he shot an incredible ten clay pigeons in 2.2 seconds using the Benelli ComforTech M2 Field gun.

Cordoba 12-gauge synthetic

Legacy 12-gauge

Legacy 20-gauge

M2 Field 12-gauge max 4

*M2 Field
12-gauge walnut*

*Montefeltro
12-gauge walnut*

*Montefeltro 20-gauge
shortstock*

Benelli

Montefeltro
20-gauge walnut

Nova pump 20-gauge
shortstock

Black Eagle II
12-gauge max 4

Black Eagle II
12-gauge synthetic

Black Eagle II
12-gauge walnut

Sport II 12-gauge
walnut

Benelli

Supernova 12-gauge steady-grip synthetic

Supernova 12-gauge comfortech synthetic

Supernova 12-gauge max 4

Supernova 12-gauge pistol grip tactical synthetic ghost ring sights

Supernova 12-gauge comfortech synthetic

Supernova 12-gauge pistol grip tactical synthetic

Benelli

Supersport 12-gauge comfortech

Supersport 20-gauge comfortech

Cordoba 12-gauge max 4

M2 field 12-gauge
APG HD

M2 field 20-gauge
comfortech APG
HD

M4 tactical
12-gauge desert

Montefeltro 12-gauge silver walnut

Nova pump 12-gauge APG HD

Rifled slug 12-gauge synthetic

Sport II 20-gauge walnut

Supertsport 20-gauge comfor-tect carbon

Super black eagle II 12-gauge slug with scope

Benelli

M2 synthetic grip
tight coating

Millionare
12-gauge

Curator 12-gauge

36

Elite 20-gauge

Exclusive
20-gauge

Nova pump tactical
synthetic

Benelli

*Legacy Sport
12-gauge walnut*

*M2 APG steadygrip
12-gauge*

*M2 tactical
comfortech +
magtube*

M3 Convertible

M4 pistol grip synthetic

Nova APG 20-gauge

Benelli

Nova pump synthetic 20-gauge

Nova pump short stock APG HD 20-gauge

Rafaello Legacy 12-gauge

*Rafaello Deluxe
12-gauge*

*Supersport per-
formance shop
20-gauge*

Vinci synthetic

Beretta

Founded in 1526, Beretta is one of the oldest corporations in the world. For almost 500 years, Beretta has been owned by the same family. The earliest bill of sale in the company archives indicates that in 1526, gunsmith Maestro Bartolomeo Beretta of Gardone Val Trompia (Brescia, Lombardy, Italy) sold 185 arquebus (heavy musket needing to be propped up by supports) barrels to the Arsenal of Venice. Over the span of nearly five centuries, Beretta developed from a small guild operation making exquisitely detailed and precision-handmade firearms to an international firm trading in more than 100 countries and using the most modern forms of manufacture, including robotics.

By the twentieth century, the company was producing both military and sporting firearms. This marked the onset of decades of incredible growth. At the end of the nineteenth century, Beretta had 130 employees and a single 10,000-square-foot factory. By 2000, its factories took up more than 75,000 square feet of space in Gardone and another 50,000 square feet at sites in Italy, Spain, and the United States (Maryland).

During World War II, Beretta manufactured rifles and pistols for the Italian military until the 1943 Armistice between Italy and the Allied forces. The Germans still controlled the northern part of Italy, and they seized the Beretta factories and continued producing arms until 1945.

In the 1950s, Beretta expanded into automobile and motorcycle production. A true indication of its international fame came in the 1960s, however, when Ian Fleming's master spy, James Bond 007, carried a 25-caliber Beretta in both books and film.

Today, the company is owned and is run by Ugo Gussalli Beretta (a direct descendant of Bartolomeo) and his sons, Franco and Pietro. One of the world's great arms producers, Beretta makes more than 1,500 pieces each day, ranging from portable firearms (shotguns for hunting and competition, pump-action guns, semiautomatic pistols, and assault rifles). Although more than 90 percent of their production is in sporting firearms, Beretta also supplies arms to the Italian military, the U.S. Armed Forces and State Police, France's Gendarmerie Nationale and the French Air Force, the Spanish Guardia Civil, and the Turkish Police Force, among others.

The parent company, Beretta Holding, controls Beretta USA, Benelli, Franchi, SAKO, Stoeger, Tikka, Uberti, the Burris Optics Company, and 20 percent interest of the Browning arms company.

686 White Onyx

687 EELL Diamond Pigeon

AL391 Urika 2 Sporting

DT10 Skeet

SV10 Prevail

687 Silver Pigeon II

Beretta

687 Silver Pigeon III

AL391 Teknys Gold Sport

AL391 Teknys Gold Target

DT10 Trident Sport

UGB 25

DT10 Trident Trap

Beretta

471 EL

3901

AL391 Teknys Gold

Rifled Slug

Silver Hawk

Silver Pig IV

Beretta

Ultralight Classic

Ultralight Deluxe

Urika 2 Camo

48

Urika 2 Camo Max 4

Urika 2 Classic

Xtrema 2 AP

Blaser

Gunsmith Horst Blaser developed a lightweight and safe over-and-under rifle/shotgun combination, the Blaser "Diplomat." His manufacturing capacities were limited, however, and so the majority of the parts for the shotgun were produced by Ferlach in Austria. The first examples were available for sale in 1957. Typical of the Blaser emphasis on safety was the single lock with manual cocking lever with a classic claw mount. This shotgun became a popular gun for hunters.

Eventually, Blaser was able to reconfigure the Diplomat so that he could produce most of the necessary components himself, all but the barrel bore. This was the Model 60, the first German gun ever produced totally buy machines. The Model 60 evolved further to become the ES ("Einschloss" or single-lock). Both the receiver and the monoblock needed to be enlarged to permit the use of a much wider range of calibers. In 1970 the ES 70 debuted. This was the first

shotgun with interchangeable barrels so that hunters were able to fit different calibers to a single weapon. By now, Blaser was entering the international market, producing their first English language catalog.

The Blaser shotguns continued to be refined and improved with the use of new technologies and materials, and the addition of advanced mounts and scopes. Today, Blaser continues to produce safe and high-quality products along with several sidelines, including accessories and clothing.

F3 Exclusiv

F3 Super Luxus

F3 Imperial

F3 Game   *F3 Baronesse*   *F3 Standard*

F3 Competition Trap

F3 American Trap

F3 American Skeet

F3 Attache

F3 Competition Sporting

F3 Super Exclusiv

Browning

The Browning Arms Company opened in Ogden, Utah, in 1927, one year after the death of John Moses Browning, the renowned gunsmith and firearms inventor from whom the company took its name. In 1852 Jonathon Browning, father of John, had set up his first gun store in Ogden. After Jonathon's death in 1872, John Moses Browning and his five brothers established Browning Brothers Company, a retail arms business. John Browning is known as the greatest firearms inventor in history.

Browning had 128 gun patents; during his years as an inventor more than 50 million guns were produced from those patents. His best known, and most widely sold guns, included the 45-caliber pistol, the 1895 Colt Peacemaker machine gun, the Browning automatic rifle, several 30- and 50-caliber machine guns, and the Browning Automatic-5 shotgun, which was first made in 1902 and is manufactured still today. The Browning Company also became well known for other products such as gun safes, knives, and shooting and hunting apparel.

The actual production of the guns eventually was handed over to a number of firearm manufacturers, including Winchester Arms, the Colt Arms Manufacturing Company, and the Fabrique Nationale of Belgium, the Remington Arms Company, and Savage Arms Company. All of these produce guns from John Browning's patents.

The Fabrique Nationale of Belgium purchased the company in 1977, but the world headquarters is still located just outside of Ogden, Utah, in Mountain Green. By 1989 the sales for the company exceeded $100 million just in the United States. Today Browning's company catalog includes sporting rifles and guns, knives, pistols, fishing gear, outdoor clothing, and golf clubs.

Silver Hunter

Silver Rifled Deer Stalker

Silver Stalker

Silver Lightning

Browning

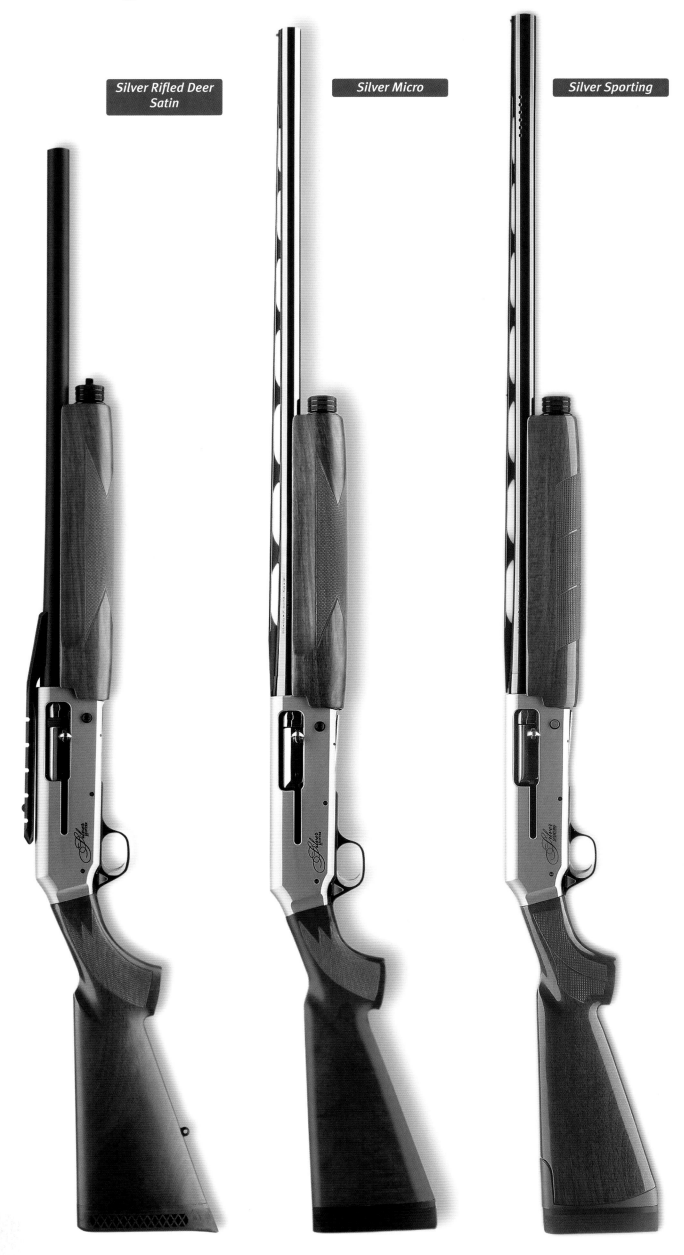

Silver Rifled Deer
Satin

Silver Micro

Silver Sporting

56

Silver Mossy Oak Tree Stand

Maxus Stalker

Maxus Mossy Oak Duck Blind

Browning

BPS Hunter

BPS Stalker

BPS Rifled Deer Hunter

BPS Micro

BPS High Capacity

Citori Superlight Feather

Browning

Citori XS Skeet

Citori Lightning

Cynergy Classic Trap

Cynergy Classic Field

Cynergy Classic Sporting

Cynergy Euro Sporting Colored Composite, Yellow

Cynergy Feather

Cynergy Euro Sporting

Cynergy Euro Field

Cynergy Satin
Composite

Citori 625
Sporting

Citori 625 Field

Browning

Citori Grand Prix Sporting

Citori Trap XT Plus Grade III

Citori Heritage

Citori One Millionth
Commemorative

Citori 625 Feather

Citori White Hunter

CZUB

The beginnings of Ceska zbrojovka Uhersky Brod (CZUB) were in 1936, when it was established as a division of Ceska zbrojovka in the town of Uhersky Brod in Czechoslovakia, now in the Czech Republic. The first firearms produced by the fledgling company were machine guns for aircraft, military pistols, and small bore rifles. During the years of Nazi Occupation during World War II, the workers at the plant were made to produce and repair weapons for the Germans. After the war, beginning in 1945, CZUB manufactured both military and civilian firearms.

In 1950 the company became a totally separate government enterprise, "Presne strojirenstvi Uhersky Brod" (Precision Machine Tooling Company), and was set up with a number of specialized subdivisions. During the decades of the Cold War, CZUB produced a range of military armaments including both rifles and pistols. Through the 1970s and 1980s, the firm was merged with other companies and worked in producing airplane engines and tractors.

By the 1990s, the company was once more an independent entity devoted to producing a range of firearms and reassuming the name Ceska zbrojovka s.p. In 1992 the joint stock company Ceska zbrojovka a.s., Uhersky Brod was established in agreement with a Czech privatization project and the decentralization of government concerns. As it joined the economy of the Free World, CZUB sold weapons in more than sixty countries. In 1997 it opened CZ-USA in the United States and continues to produce military, law enforcement, and recreational firearms. Today, CZUB has more than 2,000 employees and is one of the world's largest arms manufacturers.

BRNO 801.2

BRNO Combo

BRNO 801.1

BRNO 801.2 Fancy

BRNO Combo

Ringneck

*BRNO Stopper
Fancy*

CZUB

BRNO Stopper

Woodcock

BRNO Stopper with
hand-engraved
silver reciever

712 Semiauto

6210

Grouse

CZUB

Partridge

Ringneck deluxe

Sporting 32"

70

Sporting 30"

Woodcock deluxe

712 Utility shotgun

Bobwhite

Canvasback deluxe

Durango

Hammercoach

Mallard

Redhead deluxe

FABARM

First established in 1900, Fabbrica Bresciana Armi (FABARM) is located in Brescia, Italy. Brescia has traditionally been a center for the manufacture of Italian shotguns, with such notable firms as that of the Galesi family. FABARM has also been proud of its dedication to combining the most modern production methods with true classic craftsmanship.

Their line of firearms includes products for military, law enforcement, sportsmen, and hunters: semiautomatic shotguns, over-and-under shotguns for both hunting and exhibition shooting, side-by-side, and express rifles. Recently, FABARM has entered into a partnership with Heckler & Koch to market a wide range of shotguns in North America.

Axis 20 Elite

Axis 28 Elite

Classis grade IV

Elos A field

Elos B

Elos C Field

Elos C Sporting

FNH

FNH, formally known as Fabrique Nationale Herstal, was founded in 1889 in the small town of Herstal outside of Liege in Belgium. Today "FN" is a subsidiary of the Herstal Group which also owns U.S. Repeating Arms Company (Winchester) and Browning Arms Company.

In 1889 the company joined other arms manufacturers as a part of a company named Fabrique Nationale d'Armes de Guerre to help produce 150,000 Mauser Model 89 rifles ordered by the Belgian government.

In 1897 the company acquired the license for John Browning's 7.65 Browning pistol with its innovative locking system. This was the beginning of a long and productive collaboration between the Belgian company FN and Browning, the Utah inventor. In fact, Browning's son, Val, carries on his father's work with the company.

In the beginning of the twentieth century, FN also became involved in producing cars, motorcycles, and trucks. In 1914 the two bullets that killed the Archduke Ferdinand and set off World War I came from an FN Model 1910 semiautomatic pistol in 7.65 x 17 mm (.32 ACP).

In the 1930s, Browning designed his renowned .50 Cal M2 machine gun which is still manufactured by FN today.

In the later part of the twentieth century, FN helped to develop and produce both machine guns and light rifles used by NATO forces. Through to the present day, FN has continued to develop and produce innovative firearms and weapons systems that are deployed by the military by land, sea, and air.

FN Self-loading Police Gun

FN SLP Mark I Rifled Barrel

FN Tactical Police Shotgun with collapsible stock

SLP Tactical

Franchi

Franchi SpA is located in the city of Brescia, Italy, historically important as an area of gunmakers. Franchi began producing firearms in 1868 based on their expertise not only in gunsmithing but also in refining ores and metalworking. The driving philosophy of the Franchi company has been continual innovation which has resulted in major developments in the technology of gunmaking.

In recent years, Franchi has produced and developed multi-barreled sets of over-and-under shotguns, and a new simple, reliable, gas-operated auto-loader.

I-12 Upland Hunter

720 Waterfowl

720 Competition

720 Weathercoat

Destino

Highlander

Renaissance
Sporting

Franchi

48 AL Deluxe

48 AL Field

720 Advantage Max 4

720 Shortstock

I-12 Limited

I-12 Realtree

Franchi

I-12 Sporting

I-12 Max 4

I-12 Standard

82

I-12 Synthetic

720 Raptor

Renaissance Field

Harrington & Richardson

In 1871, Gilbert Harrington invented the top-breaking shell-ejecting revolver, providing a firearm that was not only both accurate and durable, but it had the added value of being easy to load and unload. In order to manufacture this new revolver, Harrington teamed with William Richardson to form Harrington & Richardson.

By 1893 the company's success allowed them to build a new plant in Worcester, Massachusetts. This enabled them to develop and produce a successful and revolutionary line of single-barrel shotguns with automatic shell ejection features.

During World War I, Harrington & Richardson manufactured shoulder-held flare guns for the military. In 1932 a new pistol record was established using a Harrington & Richardson single-shot target pistol which was later adopted for use by the United States Army. The company became a main provider of firearms for United States armed forces during World War II, manufacturing the M1 Garand rifle, the M14, and the M16.

In 1986 the company went out of business and a new firm was formed, Harrington & Richardson 1871. In 2000 Harrington & Richardson was purchased by Marlin Firearms Company. Today, Harrington & Richardson 1871 is part of the Remington Arms Company family, manufacturing several lines of firearms, particularly single-shot shotguns under two trademarks, New England Firearms and Harrington & Richardson.

Pardner Pump Field Gun

Pardner Turkey Matte Black

Pardner Compact

Pardner With Screw-in Choke

Topper Classic Junior

Topper Deluxe

Topper Trap Gun

Ultra Slug Hunter Deluxe

Ultra Slug Hunter

NEF Excell Auto Synthetic

NEF Excell Auto Turkey

Pardner Pump Walnut

Harrington & Richardson

Pardner Pump Turkey

Pardner Pump Turkey — Full Camo Dip

Pardner Pump Cantilever Slug Gun

Pardner Waterfowl

Ultra Light Slug Hunter

Ultra Slug Hunter Thumbhole Stock

Marocchi

In 1926 Stefano Marocchi began his gun manufacturing in the Trompia Valley north of Brescia, an area that has been renowned for weapons manufacturing since Roman times. Most major Italian gun manufacturers have established their headquarters in this area.

Marocchi began with a small workshop but soon gained awards for the development of a new system for a CO2 operating rifle. At the Inventor's Salon in 1961, he won a gold medal for his patent on a pistol and gun for underwater fishing.

His son, Pietro, further expanded the company in 1972 with the addition of a new facility in Sarezzo. Being a world-class shooter gave Pietro unique insights into what was needed in the competitive shooting field of the time. He conceived the Conquista or Contrast models, which became some the best firearms in the competitive shooting area.

Today, still in the hands of the original family, the firm is headed by Mauro Marocchi (Pietro Marocchi's son) and his son, Michele.

Model 100 All-Weather

Model 03 Trap

A12 Limited Edition

A12 Synthetic

Tecno Gold

SI12 Wood

SI12 Complus

Mossberg

In 1919, Oscar Frederick Mossberg along with his sons, Iver and Harold, established O. F. Mossberg & Sons, Inc. The company initially produced a .22-caliber handgun nicknamed the "Brownie." There followed in quick succession Brownie .22 caliber rifles, shotguns, and rifle scopes. The product line was increasingly diversified to include golf clubs, gun racks, campers, and sailboats.

Over the years, the company continued to develop innovative new products and techniques: Monte Carlo–type stocks, molded trigger housings, and spring-loaded quick-release swivels. O. F. Mossberg & Sons, Inc. is not only the oldest family-controlled

firearms manufacturer in the United States but also the world's largest producer of pump-action shotguns.

Still under family control today, the company manufactures such popular and industry-standard firearms for home security, personal protection, military, and law enforcement uses.

500 Bantam Black Synthetic

500 Bantam Wood Stock 12-Gauge 24"

500 Bantam Wood Stock 20-Gauge 22"

505 Youth Wood Stock 20-Gauge 20"

505 Youth Wood Stock .410 Bore 20"

500 Field Wood Stock
.410 Bore

500 Flyway Max 4
12-Gauge 28"

500 Grand Slam Turkey Break-Up Camo
12-Gauge 20"

500 Slugster Break Up
Camo 12-Gauge 24"

500 Turkey Tactical
12-Gauge

500 Muzzleloader
Wood .50 24"

500 S 12-Gauge Camo 24"

500 Field 12-Gauge Synthetic 28"

500 Tactical turkey 12-Gauge Synthetic

Mossberg

535 ATS Thumbhole
Turkey 12-Gauge 20"
Synthetic

535 ATS Thumbhole
Turkey 12-Gauge 20"
Break-Up Camo

535 ATS Slugster
12-Gauge Synthetic
24"

535 ATS Tactical Turkey 12-Gauge 24" Break-Up Camo

835 Ulti Mag Waterfowl 12-Gauge 28" Wood

835 Ulti Mag Tactical Turkey 12-Gauge 20" Break-Up Camo

Mossberg

930 Field 12-Gauge
Walnut 26"

930 Pistol Gripp
Turkey 12-Gauge
Synthetic 24"

Silver Reserve Field
12-Gauge Walnut 28"

Silver Reserve Side-By-Side 28-Gauge Walnut 26"

SA-20 Bantam 20-Gauge Synthetic 24"

930SX 12-Gauge Synthetic 18.5"

Remington

According to legend, in 1816 Eliphalet Remington II believed he could build a better gun than he could buy, and so he set out to do just that. Even though he came in second in a shooting competition with his homemade flintlock rifle, other contestants wanted to buy it. In 1828, his gun business had outgrown his workshop in his hometown of Ilion Gorge, New York. He started a new facility in Ilion, close to the recently opened Erie Canal. The site of that early facility is still home to a Remington arms factory today.

The Remington Company was responsible for the design and implementation of the first hammerless solid-breech repeating shotgun, and hammerless auto-loading shotgun. They also manufactured the first successful high-power slide-action repeating rifle and lock-breech auto-loading rifle. As business continued to grow, in 1865 Remington incorporated and took on stockholders. In 1873, he expanded his product line and began manufacturing typewriters. Eventually the company split into Remington Rand, later Sperry Rand (which produced the typewriters), and the Remington Arms Company. Remington sold the typewriter business in 1886.

Marcus Hartley and Partners, a large sporting goods firm bought Remington Arms in 1888 and opened a second facility in Bridgeport, Connecticut. In 1912, Remington merged with another Hartley company, Union Metallic Cartridge to form Remington UMC.

During World War I, Remington increased manufacturing facilities, and after the war, to take full advantage of these new capabilities, Remington began making pocket and hunting knives, household utensils, and cash registers. They created a cloth patch with their logo for marketing purposes, and this eventually developed into yet another product line, clothing.

Prior to World War II, Remington worked in collaboration with the United States government to expand ammunition and arms production. In 1940, Remington was asked to construct new production plants in Salt Lake City, Utah; Denver, Colorado; Lake City, Minnesota; King Mills, Ohio; and Lowell, Massachusetts. Although the plants were owned by the government, they were operated by Remington.

Until the present day, Remington continues to bring out innovative lines of rifles and shotguns, ammunition, accessories and clay pigeons, and to expand their production facilities throughout the country.

870 Compact Camo

870 Tac Grey

887 NitroMag

870 Tac Ghost

870 Super Slug

870 Compact Pink

887 Nitro Black

M870 Compact

1187 Super Cell

Model 332   SPR220   SPR310

Model 105 CTI II

Model 1100 Premier Sporting

Model 1100 TAC-4

SPR210 Cowboy

SPR310

SP-10 Magnum

Rossi

Amadeo Rossi established the Rossi Company in 1889. The founder's goal was to produce an affordable product without giving up an accuracy or quality in Sao Paolo, Brazil.

In 1997, in order to better control their sales, Rossi set up BrazTech International as an exclusive importer of Rossi products in North America.

Rossi is known for the production of revolvers, single-shot rifles, muzzleloaders, and lever-action rifles. In 2003 Rossi was honored with the awards of "Best of the Best" and "Best Value" from *Field & Stream* magazine for its Rossi Trifecta. The versatile Trifecta is like three guns in one, as the system includes barrels for a .243 Winchester, 22 Long Rifle, and a 20-gauge shotgun.

Rossi is still in the hands of the original family.

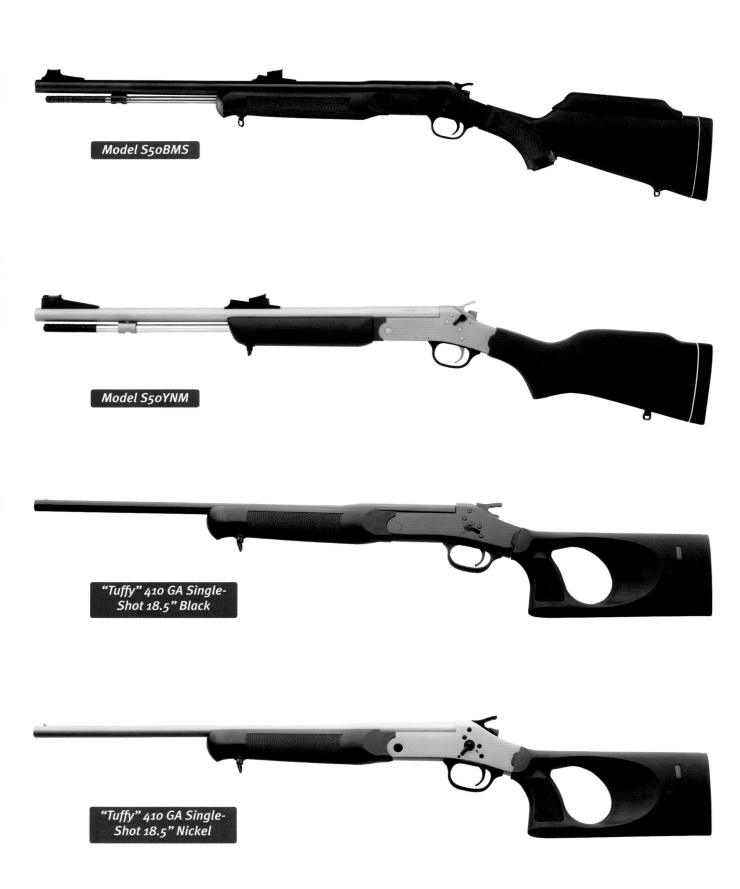

Model S50BMS

Model S50YNM

"Tuffy" 410 GA Single-Shot 18.5" Black

"Tuffy" 410 GA Single-Shot 18.5" Nickel

Rifled Barrel Slug Gun

Turkey Gun

Full-Size Field

Ruger

Ruger (the common name for Sturm, Ruger & Co.) is the largest maker of firearms in the United States, as well as one of the few to make all three major lines of firearms: handguns, shotguns, and rifles. Their corporate motto is, "Arms Makers for Responsible Citizens."

Founded by William B. Ruger and Alexander McCormick Sturm in 1949 in a small rented machine shop in Southport, Connecticut, it first produced a well-received 22-caliber pistol. Some of the design features of the pistol came out of Ruger's earlier work studying and adapting techniques from two Baby Nambu pistols he had recieved from a United States Marine who had brought them home from Japan after World War II. Although the company decided not to market the actual pistols, they did use the Nambu's rear-style cocking device and silhouette in the concept for the .22 caliber pistols.

Ruger has been an important manufacturer of the .22 rimfire rifle with their popular Ruger 10/22. Sales can be credited to its relative low cost and good quality combined with a large number of accessories and available parts. Ruger also has a large share of the .22 rimfire semiautomatic pistol market.

In 1951 Alex Sturm died, and the company continued to be run by William B. Ruger until his death in 2002. Since 1969, Sturm, Ruger has been a public company and, in 1990, became a New York Stock Exchange company.

Between 1949 and 2004, Ruger produced and marketed more than 20 million firearms. Today Ruger manufactures and distributes a wide range of firearms for use in hunting, target shooting, self-defense, collecting, and law enforcement.

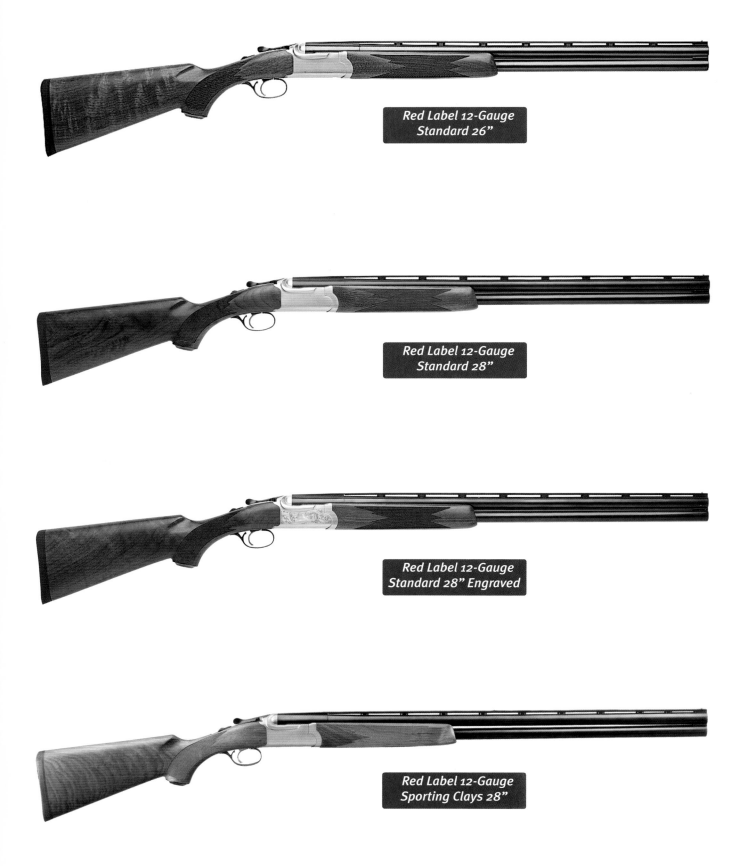

Red Label 12-Gauge
Standard 26"

Red Label 12-Gauge
Standard 28"

Red Label 12-Gauge
Standard 28" Engraved

Red Label 12-Gauge
Sporting Clays 28"

Red Label 20-Gauge
Pistol Grip 26"

Red Label 20-Gauge
Straight English 26"

Red Label 28-Gauge
Pistol Grip 28"

Stoeger

The Stoeger name in connection with fine-quality handguns began in 1923. At that time, an Austrian immigrant to the United States, Alexander F. Stoeger, opened a shop in New York City. He listed himself as the exclusive importer of Mauser and Lugers Arms and Ammunition into the United States and Canada. By 1924 Stoeger already was able to distribute a marketing and sales catalog.

The Finnish arms manufacturer, Sako, bought out Stoeger in the 1990s. In less than ten years, Sako was purchased by Beretta Holdings. Beretta put Stoeger under their subsidiary, Benelli USA.

Condor Outback
12-Gauge Black/Nickel

Condor Outback
12-Gauge Walnut/Blue

Condor Outback
20-Gauge Black/Nickel

Condor Outback
20-Gauge Walnut/Blue

M2000 12-Gauge
APG HD

M2000 12-Gauge
Synthetic

M2000 12-Gauge
Max 4

M2000 12-Gauge
Satin/Walnut

M2000 12-Gauge
Timber

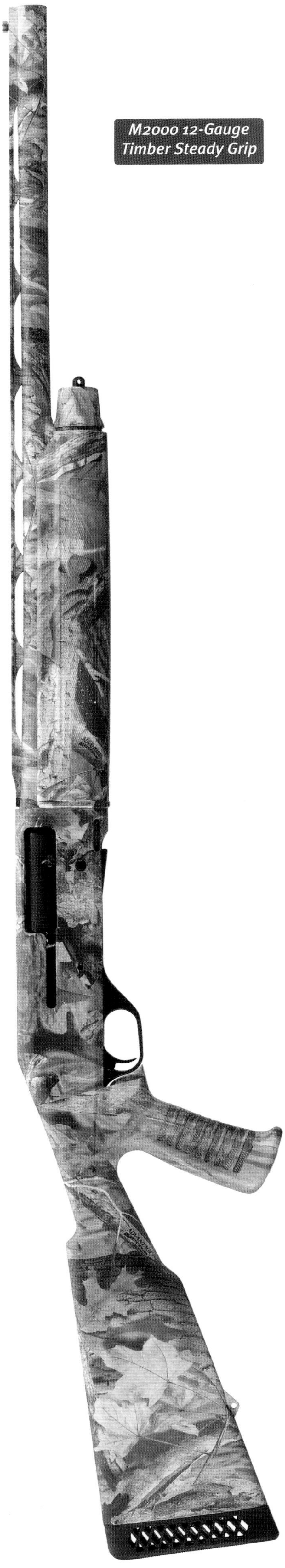

M2000 12-Gauge
Timber Steady Grip

M2000 12-Gauge Defense Steady Grip

MP-350 12-Gauge APG HD

Coach Gun Nickel

Stoeger

Coach Silverado English Stock

Coach Supreme Blue Stainless

Coach Supreme Blue

Coach Supreme
Nickel

Coach Standard

Condor Competition
12-Gauge

Stoeger

Condor Competition 20-Gauge

Condor Special

Condor Supreme

Condor Youth

Condor Standard

*M2000 APG
Camo Steady Grip
12-Gauge*

MP-350 APG Steady Grip 12-Gauge

MP-350 Synthetic Steady Grip 12-Gauge

MP-350 Max 4 12-Gauge

MP-350 Synthetic Pistol Grip 12-Gauge

MP-350 Synthetic 12-Gauge

MP-350 Timber 12-Gauge

Stoeger

Single Barrel Classic

Single Barrel Special

Uplander Special

Uplander Supreme

Single Barrel Classic Youth

Uplander Standard

Thompson/Center

Thompson/Center Arms Company was set up in 1965 when a convenient colloboration between K. W. Thompson Tool Company, which was seeking new products to fill its production capabilities, partnered with Warren Center, a gun designer in search of a manufacturer for his Contender pistol. Thompson Tool facilities were expanded and the new company, Thompson/Center, was formed in Rochester, New Hampshire. It took only two years for the first Contender pistols to ship, and the company has been producing hunting handguns ever since. Today, Thompson/Center has marketed more than 400,000 of these pistols.

Two years later, the first contender pistol was shipped, starting a trend in high-performance hunting handguns, which continues to grow every year. To date, over 400,000 Contender pistols have been shipped and the pistol's reputation for versatility, accuracy, and dependability goes unchallenged among serious handgun shooters.

The company became known for its line of interchangeable barrel single-shot pistols and rifles. The company has also helped spur a resurgance of interest in muzzle-loading rifles, which they began manufacturing in 1970 with the introduction of the Hawken Muzzleloading rifle.

In the present day, Thompson/Center's product line includes single-shot pistols and rifles, and a full line of muzzleloading rifles and accessories. The original version of the Contender pistol has been updated as the G2 Contender and is one of the best-known hunting handguns available today.

Encore Rifled Slug Gun
20-Gauge Blued Walnut

Encore Shotgun
12-Gauge Blued Walnut

Encore Shotgun
20-Gauge Blued Walnut

Encore 28" Stainless Fluted

Encore Slug Gun 12-Gauge Blued Walnut

Encore Turkey Gun 20-Gauge Realtree

Verney-Carron

In 1820, the twenty-year-old Claude Verney entered one of his own handmade guns in the celebrated gunmaking competition in Saint Etienne, France, Concours d'Armurerie. In the early nineteenth century, Saint Etienne, located in the Massif Central region of eastern central France, was the acknowledged arms-making center of the country. His winning entry was described as "a magnificent mounting on a heavily carved gun stock." Today, his winning gun can be seen in the Museum of Art and Industry in Saint Etienne.

Verney was a fifth-generation gunmaker with family ties going back in the firearms business to his great-great-grandfather, Guy Verney, in 1650. In addition, most of Verney's male ancestors had married daughters of gunmakers. Verney wasted little time in taking the most advantage of his victory; he launched his own firearms company in that very year.

The company continues to use its well-known Sagittarius logo, giving its name to one of the company's main series of guns, the Sagittaire. This line was launched in 1967 and is the standard for modern Verney-Carron products. Verney-Carron followed this success with the Super 9 Trap in 1988 and a featherweight model, the Plume, in 1993.

Almost 200 years later, the headquarters and workshops of Verney-Carron's take up nearly 54,000 square feet at the intersection of Boulevard Thiers and Rue de Verney-Carron. The company is one of the largest businesses in St. Etienne. Verney-Carron produces a remarkable array of sporting guns. The company is run by the sixth-generation member of Verney family, headed by Pierre Verney-Carron, president. Verney-Carron is one of the few firearms makers who produce all barrels in-house combining high-grade steel with chrome and molybdenum. In mountains above Saint Etienne sits L'Atelier Verney-Carron, the company's custom gun shop where fifteen craftsmen design and build custom-crafted guns.

Vercar Side By Side 12-Gauge

Vercar Side By Side 20-Gauge

Vercar Side By Side Canardouze

Sagittaire Becassier

Verney-Carron

Sagittaire Gros
Gibier 12-Gauge

Sagittaire Le
Billebaude

Sagittaire Le
Mordoree

Sagittaire Mixte Classique

Sagittaire One

Sagittaire Polynox Classique

Verney-Carron

Sagittaire Polynox
Extra-Luxe

Semiauto Vercar
Wood

Semiauto Vercar
Synthetic

Super 9 Prestige

Super 9 Sport Parcours De Chasse

Super 9 Sport Trap

Verney-Carron

Super 9 Super-
charge Luxe

Super 9 Grand Be-
cassier Extra Luxe

Super 9 Plume

Super 9 Prestige

Super 9 Super
Leger Extra Luxe

Superpose Vercar

Weatherby

In 1945, Roy Weatherby set up his arms company in order to produce guns to his concept that lightweight bullets moving at very fast speeds were the best for one-shot kills. He spent the next ten years perfecting high-powered Weatherby Magnum cartridges. The company is still known for these cartridges. He also designed and produced rifles that were specifically equipped to handle his new type of ammunition.

In 1957, he developed a new gun, the Mark V, which was a stronger, safer weapon able to stand up to great pressure. Then again in 1970, he conceived another innovative product the Weatherby Vanguard, with many of the traits of the Mark V but with two locking lugs.

In 1983, Weatherby's son, Ed, took over the company and has overseen the expansion of the Mark V and Vanguard lines of weapons as well as adding semiautomatic, pump, side-by-side, and over/under shotguns. All support lines of accompanying accessories, in addition to a line of apparel and collectibles.

*Athena Di'Italia III
Over-and-Under*

*Athena Di'Italia IV
Over-and-Under*

Athena Di'Italia PG

Athena Di'Italia

Athena Di'Italia V
Over-and-Under

Orion Di'Italia I
Over-and-Under

Orion Di'Italia II
Over-and-Under

Weatherby

Orion Di'Italia III
Over-and-Under

Orion Di'Italia

Orion Di'Italia SC

PA-08 Synthetic

PA-08 Upland

PA-459

Weatherby

SA-08 Deluxe

SA-08 Synthetic Youth

SA-08 Synthetic

SA-08 Waterfowler 3.0

SA-08 Upland

SA-08 Youth

Winchester

In 1855, Horace Smith and Dan Wesson established Volcanic Repeating Arms Company in Norwich, Connecticut, in order to produce their Volcanic lever-action rifle. In 1856, the company was renamed the New Haven Arms company and moved to that city. The Volcanic rifle used Hunt's Rocket Ball ammunition and did not meet with any great commercial success. Eventually B. T. Henry redesigned the gun to allow it to use different ammunition, and it became known as the Henry rifle. In 1862, the first Henry rifles were sold and used in large numbers by the Union forces during the Civil War.

In 1866, Oliver Winchester bought control of New Haven Arms Company and changed its name to Winchester Repeating Arms Company. The first gun to have the Winchester name was the Model 1866 Yellow Boy lever action.

In the 1880s, John Browning collaborated with the Winchester firm to formulate and build a series of repeating rifles and shotguns that included the Winchester Model 1885 Single-Shot, Winchester Model 1887 lever-action shotgun, Model 1897 pump-action shotgun, and Model 1895 (with a box magazine) rifle.

By the beginning of the twentieth century, however, Winchester Repeating Arms was actually in competition with new John Browning designs manufactured by several other companies. There was heated competition during this period to devise the first commercially viable self-loading rifle. Winchester produced the .22 rimfire Winchester Model 1903, as well as several later models.

In 1911, Winchester brought out its first semi-automatic shotgun, which was followed in the next year by a pump-action shotgun. The first bolt-action rifle was introduced in 1919. Yet another first was the 1930 production of a side-by-side.

With the advent of World War I, the company was a main supplier of the Enfield rifles to both the United States and British governments. Unfortunately, heavy borrowing during the war to support the necessary increase in production capabilities left the company nearly bankrupt, and in 1931, Winchester Repeating Arms was purchased by Olin Industries.

In World War II, they produced the M1 Garand rifle and later manufactured the M14 rifle.

The rest of the twentieth century was a time of financial upheaval for the firm. At the beginning of 2006, U.S. Repeating Arms, as Winchester had been renamed, announced the closing of the New Haven plant where the first Winchester arms had been produced more than 140 years earlier. Later that same year, Olin Industries stated that the Winchester product line would be built by Browning, a subsidiary of FN Herstal.

Super X3 Composite

Super X3 Walnut Field

Super X3 All-Purpose Field

Super X3 Cantilever Deer

Super X3 Water-
fowl

Super X3 NWTF
Cantilever Extreme
Turkey

Super X3 Classic
Field

Winchester

Super X3 Flanigun Exhibition/Sporting

Super X3 Gray Shadow

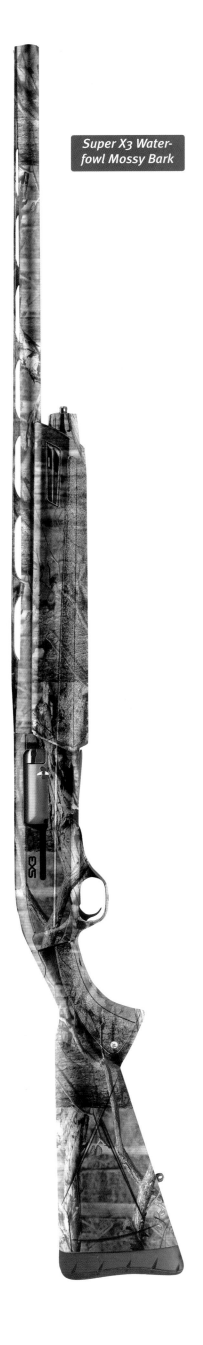

Super X3 Water-fowl Mossy Bark

Super X Pump
Black Shadow
Field

Model 101 Field

Deluxe Field

Super X Pump Defender

Model 101 Sporting

Model 101 Pigeon Grade Trap

*Model 101
Pigeon Grade
Trap Adjustable
Comb*

Model 101 Light

*Model 101
Pigeon Sporting*

Index